THE PRINCIPLES OF DEMOCRACY

WHAT IS EQUALITY?

JOSHUA TURNER

PowerKiDS press

New York

Published in 2020 by The Rosen Publishing Group, Inc.
29 East 21st Street, New York, NY 10010

Copyright © 2020 by The Rosen Publishing Group, Inc.

All rights reserved. No part of this book may be reproduced in any form without permission in writing from the publisher, except by a reviewer.

First Edition

Editor: Melissa Raé Shofner
Book Design: Reann Nye

Photo Credits: Seriest art Bplanet/Shutterstock.com; cover Jose Luis Pelaez Inc/DigitalVision/Getty Images; p. 5 Dave Nagel/Stone/Getty Images; p. 7 Everett Historical/Shutterstock.com; p. 9 Robert W. Kelley/The LIFE Picture Collection/Getty Images; p. 11 John Fedele/Blend Images/Getty Images; p. 13 Blend Images/Shutterstock.com; p. 15 Hero Images/Getty Images; p. 17 https://commons.wikimedia.org/wiki/File:1944_portrait_of_FDR_(1).jpg; p.19 AZAM Jean-Paul/hemis.fr/Getty Images; p. 21 gradyreese/E+/Getty Images; p. 22 wavebreakmedia/Shutterstock.com.

Cataloging-in-Publication Data

Names: Turner, Joshua.
Title: What is equality? / Joshua Turner.
Description: New York : PowerKids Press, 2020. | Series: The principles of democracy | Includes glossary and index.
Identifiers: ISBN 9781538342688 (pbk.) | ISBN 9781538342701 (library bound) | ISBN 9781538342695 (6 pack)
Subjects: LCSH: Equality-Juvenile literature. | Toleration-Juvenile literature.
Classification: LCC HM821.T87 2019 | DDC 305-dc23

Manufactured in the United States of America

CPSIA Compliance Information: Batch #CWPK19: For Further Information contact Rosen Publishing, New York, New York at 1-800-237-9932

CONTENTS

WHAT IS EQUALITY?............ 4
GENDER EQUALITY 6
SOCIAL EQUALITY 8
ECONOMIC EQUALITY 10
BEING EQUAL IN A DEMOCRACY ...12
CAN EVERYONE BE EQUAL?......14
INEQUALITY.................16
EXTREME EQUALITY 18
WHAT KIND OF SOCIETY
   WOULD YOU WANT? 20
EQUALITY IN EVERYDAY LIFE.....22
GLOSSARY 23
INDEX 24
WEBSITES 24

WHAT IS EQUALITY?

Imagine you and a group of friends have been asked to do a task by your teacher. The group consists of boys and girls of different ages and social **backgrounds**. Every person in your group works hard, puts in a good effort, and accomplishes the task.

Your teacher decides that because everyone did a good job you should all get a snack. The same snack will be given to everyone because you all did the same thing. That's equality.

THE SPIRIT OF DEMOCRACY

The **Enlightenment** in Europe was one of the first times a society tried to make rights equal for everyone. From the Enlightenment, we got a democracy that gives all people an equal voice in their government.

Equality means everyone will be treated fairly based on what they do and how well they do it.

5

GENDER EQUALITY

Gender equality means every person, **regardless** of their gender, gets an equal chance to succeed. It doesn't matter if you're a man or a woman—everyone gets the chance to go to school, get a job, vote in an election, or even run for office themselves.

Women and men haven't always been equal under the law. In many places, they still don't have equality. The United States has come a long way in creating equal opportunities for both men and women to succeed.

> Susan B. Anthony was one of the first women to fight for women's equality. With her help, women were granted voting rights equal to those of men in 1920.

SOCIAL EQUALITY

Social equality is about respecting and **appreciating** everyone for everything they bring to a society. Movements—such as those for civil rights—have helped create equal opportunities for everyone to succeed.

In a democracy, a person's social standing shouldn't matter when we think about what they can contribute, or give, to society and the respect they should be given. Learning about how all people play a role in society helps create a world with greater social equality.

THE SPIRIT OF DEMOCRACY

Martin Luther King Jr. fought for social equality in the 1950s and 1960s. He believed blacks and whites should be able to attend the same schools, work in the same jobs, and be treated the same by police.

Respect for everyone and equality before the law are key ideas in social equality.

9

ECONOMIC EQUALITY

Economics is about more than money. It's also about how goods and services are created, sold, and purchased. The value of someone's money, property, and **possessions** is called wealth.

Economic equality is the idea that everyone in a society should have a fair and equal chance at **obtaining** wealth. Income inequality, or the uneven spread of money across a society, often gets in the way of economic equality. Wage inequality—such as how women sometimes earn less money than men who do the same jobs—does, too.

> In the United States, it's often said that the rich are getting richer and the poor are getting poorer. This income inequality keeps America from having economic equality.

BEING EQUAL IN A DEMOCRACY

What does it mean to be equal in a democracy? Most importantly, it means every person—no matter their gender, social status, or wealth—gets to vote, and every person's vote counts the same.

Equality in a democracy can also mean that every person gets a good education. A good education helps people be **informed** so they can make good decisions, know who they're voting for and why, and take part in society.

THE SPIRIT OF DEMOCRACY

France was one of the first countries in Europe to give its citizens the right to vote and choose their leaders. Today, France is one of the greatest democracies in the world.

With equality, everyone's vote counts the same—even the president's. The ability to vote is what being equal in a democracy is all about.

13

CAN EVERYONE BE EQUAL?

Everyone can be equal, but not in exactly the same way. Think about your own classroom. Some students are good at math, some are good at reading, and some are good at science.

These students aren't equal in exactly what they know, but they're equal in what they're able to bring to the classroom and in the respect they **deserve** for their effort. Being equal doesn't mean being the same—it means everyone's abilities and differences are **acknowledged** and respected.

> Being equal doesn't mean everyone is exactly the same, but it does mean everyone is able to bring something important to the group.

15

INEQUALITY

Inequality occurs when some people have more rights or better opportunities than others. These differences between people can be harmful and unfair.

In a democracy, it's important to know when inequality occurs so changes can be made. This could mean passing laws, **donating** time or money, or simply talking to people to spread awareness. Inequality can be bad, but it can be fixed. In a democracy, where everyone has a voice, it can be changed through hard work.

THE SPIRIT OF DEMOCRACY

Whether it be women's rights, workers' rights, or civil rights, people in a democracy have a long and proud history of making the United States a more equal place for everyone.

President Franklin D. Roosevelt was one of the first presidents to try to fix American inequality with the New Deal program.

EXTREME EQUALITY

A democracy is a government for the people, by the people. The United States is a **representative** democracy, which means the people choose representatives to speak for them in government.

Extreme equality happens when people decide they want to be equal in every way. This includes getting rid of their representatives and handling their government directly. If everyone tries to have an equal hand in running the government, democracy will stop working. At this point, a single, all-powerful—and often unfair—leader called a despot might rise.

> Montesquieu was a great thinker of the eighteenth century. He explored the idea of extreme equality in his book *The Spirit of Laws*. His ideas helped shape the U.S. government.

WHAT KIND OF SOCIETY WOULD YOU WANT?

It's important to consider society as a whole when thinking about equality. What kind of society do you want to live in? Do you want a society in which everyone is respected and able to work hard and have his or her work acknowledged?

Or do you want a less equal society in which talented, hardworking people get much more than others. Take a moment to think about your ideal society. Keep in mind no society is perfect, and there are no real right answers.

THE SPIRIT OF DEMOCRACY

The United Nations Human Rights Council is a group that helps to make sure people around the world have equal rights and the ability to live happy, healthy lives.

Thinking about what kind of society you want is a great way to figure out what equality means to you.

EQUALITY IN EVERYDAY LIFE

⋆⋆⋆⋆⋆⋆⋆⋆⋆⋆

Almost every day you'll be faced with **situations** or decisions that have to do with equality in some way. How will you treat the people around you? How are people paid for their work? Are new laws that are passed fair for everyone?

Some parts of equality in everyday life aren't in your control, but some are. Understanding how equality affects you and those around you is one of the most important parts of living in an equal democracy.

GLOSSARY

acknowledge: To say that you accept or do not deny the truth or existence of something.

appreciate: To admire and value someone or something.

background: The experiences, knowledge, and education in a person's past.

deserve: Used to say that someone should or should not have or be given something.

donate: To give something in order to help a person or organization.

Enlightenment: A movement in the eighteenth century marked by the rejection of traditional beliefs in favor of logic and science.

gender: The state of being male or female.

informed: Having knowledge.

obtain: To gain or get something, usually by effort.

possession: Something that is owned by someone.

regardless: Without being stopped or affected by something.

representative: Someone who acts or speaks for or in support of another person or group.

situation: All the facts, conditions, and events that affect someone or something in a certain time and place.

INDEX

B
backgrounds, 4

C
civil rights, 8

E
economics, 10
education, 12

G
gender, 6, 12

I
inequality, 16

R
representatives, 18
respect, 8, 14, 20

S
social standing, 4, 8, 12

V
voting, 12

W
wealth, 10, 12

WEBSITES

Due to the changing nature of Internet links, PowerKids Press has developed an online list of websites related to the subject of this book. This site is updated regularly. Please use this link to access the list: www.powerkidslinks.com/pofd/equ

24